AN ADDRESS

DELIVERED BY

Rev. E. Benjamin Andrews,

Tuesday Evening, December 21, 1875,

AT HIS INAUGURATION AS

PRESIDENT OF DENISON UNIVERSITY,

GRANVILLE, OHIO.

COLUMBUS:
NEVINS & MYERS, BOOK PRINTERS.
1876.

DENOMINATIONAL vs. STATE COLLEGES.

We are met as patrons and lovers of a Christian college. This college, so dear to us, represents a very large class of such institutions, where good letters are cultivated in close and tender fellowship with Christian faith. These institutions are so numerous and so influential among us, as to constitute a distinguishing feature of American society. Their past history, no one can deny, has been prodigal of benign results. They have bred the best intelligence and the best manhood that America ever knew. Their importance in the present, though not obtrusive or a common subject of remark, is greater than can be calculated; and their offices are wholesome and saving to politics, learning, and religion alike.

But what is to be their destiny? It cannot but have an important bearing upon our future activity in behalf of Denison University, to consider this question, and, if possible, at least for ourselves, to decide it. The air of our day is ringing with the outcry that these institutions have fulfilled their humble temporary mission, and must now make place for better ones established by the state. An address by President White, of Cornell University, delivered before the American Educational Association at Detroit, in August, 1874, advocated such a view with remarkable boldness, ingenuity, and eloquence. His speech found the public ear quick with eagerness to listen. A large assembly of prominent educators waited, with enthusiastic attention, upon its very delivery. Reports of it, more or less complete, crowded the columns of the national press for many a day. A prominent literary periodical published it in full. A separate edition reached the people in pamphlet form. Distinguished editors, with how much deliberation it is impossible to say, hailed President White as an inspired educational reformer. Scarcely has the atmosphere stirred since then without bearing to us some echo of the memorable words at Detroit. And now, in the last number of the North American Review, comes forward Mr. Charles K. Adams with a long and able article, advocating essentially the same proposition advanced by President White, that the government, at least in the newer states, must possess control of education in its higher as well as in its lower forms.

There is no time to examine articulately the considerations by which the propriety of such a policy is sought to be established. The evils which these reformers bemoan are patent to all. The high benefits of personal freedom and development, arising from committing their chief interests to individuals themselves, are purchased at the cost of some infelicities; some positive evils. Among many others of these is this, that our colleges have become too numerous. Against England's four, and Prussia's eight universities, the United States can match above three hundred and sixty establishments titled universities or colleges. The result is that a majority of these are cursed with poverty. Faculties are too small and too poorly paid. Libraries are inadequate; apparatus, laboratories, and cabinets, are supplied in nothing like due abundance; and the most faithful and capable of professors in many chairs are forced to toil at deplorable disadvantage.

Now there is no denying that a system of state higher education might remedy these evils in part. At the same time, the conviction in me is strong that it could never heal them utterly, and that in attempting to effect this, it would be certain to occasion other worse ones; for I believe that governmental management of higher education is, in America, impracticable in fact, and every where wrong in principle. These two things I shall seek to show in their order, viewing the subject first as it regards policy or the question what *can* be done, and then as it regards principle or the question what *ought* to be done.

To proceed, then: state control of liberal education is incompatible with our republican conditions. The exigences of a free and generous government, the refuge of oppressed ones from every clime—refuge where the very air rusts off every shackle, as well of thought as of limb—the exigences of such a government force us, whether we will or not, to depend on private corporations for liberal school training. Religionists must have their seminaries of learning, and free-thinkers theirs if they want them. A state system, the very best you can devise, will fail.

For one thing, such a system would work unbearable hardship. If government assumes charge of our public instruction, what will it do with such colleges as already exist? To suppress them, or to frustrate their primary design as by converting them into state concerns neutral in religion—a course gravely proposed by some—would be monstrously wrong. The men who laid these foundations did so with the express purpose and condition that upon them learning and religion should hold eternal alliance. Those who support them now, are moved to such sacrifice by the conscientious conviction of duty to God. They believe a divinely arranged harmony to subsist between learning and religion, between the culture of the mind and the culture of the heart. Men who feel thus would regard it a sin, having it in their power, not to furnish the means to their own children, and to all others willing to profit by them, of cultivating philosophy, literature, and science, in closest connection with Christian faith. I am not now arguing that these people are right in their views of duty and propriety, but only that they are very conscientious. A strong sense of duty to God impels them to provide and to sustain Christian colleges, and it would be religious intolerance, unparalleled at least in recent American history, to deny them that privilege. Who can believe that the people will ever allow government to undertake so violent a measure?

Very few, of course, have any such wild dream. All these schools, the most of the agitators tell us, will, to be sure, be suffered to continue in their present character. Then, are the supporters of them to be taxed like other citizens to build and furnish with fuel the educational engines of the state? Here would be a hardship of another kind—not so grievous as the first, still too real and palpable to make it likely even to be imposed upon us. It requires vast sums of money to set up and equip good colleges, and whatever it costs, the consciences of Christ's followers will prompt them to provide. We may depend upon it that, however large the expense, unless suppressed by law, there are going to be noble and fully equipped Christian universities in this land, not supported out of the public purse; and unless it can be shown that costly state universities besides, erected and maintained by taxation, are absolutely indispensable to the *life* of our republic, it will be unfair in the extreme to lay upon Christian shoulders the gratuitous second burden of helping to support these. To be sure we tax Catholics for common schools, but we do it because such schools are necessary to our life as a nation. It would be cruelly wrong to do this on any other plea. So it would to do it merely as a "hopeful experiment," for *fear* that common ignorance might be harmful. We tax the whole people for lower education, because the deadliness of popular ignorance to popular government is certain, as certain as a wide induction of historical instances can make it.

But can any one soberly argue that liberal intellectual culture, such as colleges and universities are designed to give, holds any such intimate relation to the life of the government? Such a view could not be defended by the shadow of evidence. Writers fall into strange misconceptions on this point. Because liberal culture is necessary to the sovereign welfare and perfection of a *people*, it is alleged to be vital to the *state*. The two things are plainly distinct. Religion, and the Christian religion too, is essential to a a people's supreme weal. "Blessed," in the highest sense, "is that nation" alone "whose God is Jehovah." But a state, a government, can exist without the people's being all, or any of them, Christians. Common morality is enough; and so, for this other necessity, common intelligence among the masses is all that really *must* be had. And such intelligence it is the sacred duty of good government, for the sake of its own conservation, to secure, by an efficient system of common schools, with compulsory attendance, and first-rate normal schools for the adequate training of teachers. I do not say that higher culture would be of no advantage to our republic. It would, by making the people better and easier to govern. So would universal piety; but the government can do without either; it can endure though every college and university die.

But such institutions will not die. As we have seen, unless put down by law, seminaries of learning are sure to flourish. True, they may not do their work to the satisfaction of all; but while they stand, even should their effectiveness never be any greater than now, American intellectual life will continue, and no plea for state colleges on the ground of their being vital to the government, can present the remotest semblance of propriety. Hence, to double the educational burden that good men must carry, by making them help support unnecessary institutions, that they cannot patronize, and do not believe in, would be the extreme of injustice. Whether the now existing colleges be swept away, or perverted to non-religious uses, or left as they are, the erection and support by general taxation of new institutions of this character would be a grievous wrong to a large and worthy portion of the American public. We may safely depend upon the sense of justice in the people at large to forbid such a proceeding.

I argue next, that the general public is not competent to have the charge of higher education. The case is not with us as with Germany, whence our educational iconoclasts get their notions. There the sovereign power is central, and, fortunately or unfortunately, views of government prevail different from those which find favor here. The minister of education there, is not as directly responsible to the people as such a functionary would be in the United States. He can give direction to that interest according to his own intellgent will. On this side the Atlantic, the people, if they supply the funds for advanced learning, must direct the expenditure of the same. In other words, state colleges must be in politics, and be subject to all the vicissitudes of politics. You cannot set them upon any career of certain permanent progress. You cannot keep them under any fixed and definite policy. Some stubborn and ignorant legislature will be sure, sooner or later, to overturn the plans of the wisest educators. A timid legislature, frightened by the people's cry of too heavy taxation, will withhold the funds absolutely needful for proper college work. Is it said that this danger is only theoretical? Look at the history of state efforts in the direction of higher education. In how many instances have educational funds been squandered by reckless legislators? In how many cases have the people, in some moment of frenzy for retrenchment, most harmfully reduced the teaching force of a high school, or curtailed salaries beyond the possibility of retaining good teachers, or in some other way equally insane, broken hopelessly in pieces an educational policy of long standing and exceeding worth! How have political complications, from the very first, crippled the work of Girard College, and rendered that magnificent foundation almost profitless to those for whom it was laid! Take the University of Michigan, even. Is she beyond the reach of harm from popular ignorance and intractableness? One may almost say that she stands in jeopardy every hour. The people elect the regents directly, and nothing is to prevent them, at any time, from filling that office with incompetent men, and pledging them to a policy that shall be fatal to the legitimate activity of that noble seat of learning. In at least one instance already, according to Professor Ten Brook's history, has that University tottered on the very brink of ruin through the people's interference. Nor is the possibility of such meddling confined to pecuniary measures alone. It is at the option of the polls to-day, to exclude Greek from all the high schools in that state, as has already been done in Detroit. Suppose that this exclusion of Greek be made general, and that Latin share the same fate with Greek; or, that the Supreme Court by and by reverse its old decision, and ordain that the people need not be taxed for the support of high schools at all? Will not the University be hampered in her work? And then suppose the same perverse policy to be pushed, as it might be by electing ignorant and resolute demagogues for regents, into the University itself, and all liberal studies to be excluded from the academical course! I hope, indeed, that no such danger threatens, but assuredly under republican sway the suppositions just made are not wild. We have seen many such things, but we have not seen all the possible baneful developments of republicanism yet. This form of government, with all its sovereign blessings, has its drawbacks too. So mighty is the press of immigration to our shores from Catholic and heathen lands, that many, if not all of our states, may be morally and intellectually worse than now before they are better. Our present condition will not give place very soon to an educational millennium. And even were our intellectual betterment destined to go on from this time at a constant rate, the case would be much the same. Set your standard of popular intelligence as high as the most enthusiastic doctrinaire would fix it, even then what has been said will still be true: the people are not competent to direct this sovereign among the nation's interests—higher education. Doubtless the boards of private institutions are fallible, sometimes short-sighted; but stupid indeed must that man be who would not rather trust the interests of advanced education to such men, representing the higher intelligence of the Christian public, than to the great, careless rabble. Christian people are more in sympathy with advanced education, even as the reformers understand advanced education, than the general public is—more than the general public will ever be.

I next call attention to the bad economy of the measure under criticism. We cannot afford new institutions of learning, unless they are going to be better than what we now have—than what we now have give promise of being. It is suggested by President White that the denominational colleges take their places as subordinate and tributary to better institutions erected by the state, bearing to these the relation of German gymnasia to German universities. But all the likelihood is, that in time, the state concerns will be the inferior ones—inferior, at least, to many of the others. The same spirit that has led men to found these denominational establishments, and other men to sustain them, will lead still others to perfect them for usefulness. The process is already going on. Within my recollection, Wesleyan University, at Middletown, Connecticut, and our own Colby were groaning beneath mountains of poverty that threatened to crush them to death; but endowments have come, large and generous, and now, although not entirely in affluence, they are admirably equipped for noble work. Other colleges are passing through the same experience. And to this process of perfecting true and useful Christian schools, there seems destined to be no limit. Indeed, the funds are certain to pour in faster and faster as the years roll on, and the institutions prove themselves more and more worthy of Christian patronage.

Now, is state support for state colleges certain to be thus forthcoming? Critics of the present system talk as if the state would be certain to be liberal to education, if only it had that important interest in charge. Let the state build universities, and they will never lack for funds. That is the echo of every sentence pronounced in favor of state higher education. But does history warrant any such expectation concerning public liberality? We all know the answer. It is hard to raise, by taxation, money enough even for common schools, which every one admits that the state must have; and, in many a town and city, taxes for a good high school are levied and collected only by a downright battle every year. Have our state universities ever been crushed amid heaps of gold and silver? Has the word poverty never found place in their vocabulary? Have they all that money could secure of equipment in brains, buildings, and apparatus? The reply to such inquiries is at hand. Even Michigan University—and she is the most favored among state institutions—is far from being above the reach of want. If a refractory legislature, any year, should withhold the usual subsidy of from $16,000 to $20,000, that proud and noble seat of learning might be happy to partake the fare even of some schools that are fed by denominational munificence.

In view of these facts, I say it is quite unlikely that in this land, where the people are so impatient of taxation, state institutions will ever be pecuniarily as well cared for as the truly representative ones among those supported by Christian wealth. And it is still more certain that the state concerns will not, in the long run, do their work any better than the others. President White argues as if denominational colleges, by making up their faculties for the most part out of Christian men, excluded all truly accomplished and thorough-going professors from their chairs. He brings forward in illustration of this infelicity, the fact that Brown University was, of late, some time without a head, when "there were scholars, jurists, and statesmen in that commonwealth who would have done honor to the position." But did that College lose any thing by insisting that her President must be a Christian and a Baptist? No one can say so who has had the least acquaintance with the present incumbent of that office. There is not a state university in America that would not count itself happy to secure him for President. The fact is that the great denominations are not poor in distinguished savans and thinkers. If any colleges have taken up with inferior teaching talent from the mere necessity of employing Christian instructors, they have been inexcusably stupid.

Christian colleges are, then, sure, on the whole, to stand equal with any in the respects of endowment and professorial ability. There is another item in which they cannot but be superior: it is in the Christian conscientiousness with which their instruction will be given. That preceptor who looks upon his pupils as immortal beings—who feels that his teaching will be potent with results everlastingly blessed, both to the learners themselves and to an unnumbered ulterior public whom they will influence—that preceptor, I submit, cannot help being, on the whole, superior in zeal, assiduity, and impressiveness, to one who instructs, in considerable part, to display his own attainments, ridicules theistic ideas, and regards the intellects that he is fashioning as only the momentary scintillations of the great "all," destined, after a few breaths, to go out in darkness.

With these observations history agrees. State colleges thus far, and several of them have already been long upon their career among us, have not outshone the sun with the brilliancy of their educational product. Their influence, if we leave a single institution, the University of Michigan, out of the account, has been scarcely perceptible. Many denominational colleges, and youthful ones, too, can present a far more eminent record than the aged University of Virginia. Indeed, the promise of worthy results from denominational colleges must be far less fair than now, and that from state colleges far more so, before the multiplication of the latter can prove any thing else than a waste of the people's money. We cannot afford them. To establish a system of them would be the poorest economy.

As a last consideration against the feasibility of state higher education, I urge the religious complication which it would in-

volve. Christian men are jealous of their faith. Others are equally earnest that nothing shall oppose the free course of unbelief. High education must have to do with religion, and I do not believe that a great state institution of liberal learning can maintain any attiude toward religion that will not so exasperate some party or other as to make trouble at the ballot-box. President White speaks of this problem as already "wrought out;" but, in fact, we are only just beginning to confront it. Till of late Christian thinking has been overwhelmingly predominant in our country. It is so no longer. Anti-Christians are numbered by the millions, and the practice of paying state moneys for the inculcation of theistic and Christian notions, depend upon it, will not much longer remain unchallenged. The point to consider here is not that these two or three millions who reject Christianity have rights, but that they have ballots, and that their prejudices against true theism are as forcible as those of Christians in favor of the same.

Now, the instructions of a numerous and learned faculty must be either theistic or non-theistic, or partly one and partly the other. There is no realm of thought above the merest rudiments, such as are taught in common schools, where you ean avoid hearing the obtrusive echoes of the great controversy regarding theism and religion. Is the study ethics? You must decide upon an ultimate basis of right. Is it psychology? Declare whether or not thought is a secretion of the brain. Is it metaphysics? Tell me what is the authority of the causal judgment. Is it history? I ask whether there is a philosophy of history. Is it science? I must know whether matter and force are ultimate things in human thought. Education cannot be neutral on these issues without belittling itself to the character of drivel. It simply *cannot* be neutral, however hard it may try. Suppose, first, that each professor presents his subject from a theistic standpoint—the ethical doctor finding morality intuitive, and its ultimate rule, God's will; the occupant of the metaphysical chair teaching that the conception of law implies a person; and so on with all the others? Will not the great multitude of Jews, free-thinkers, atheists, pantheists, and the rest, find fault when taxes are called for to sustain such instruction? Let the overturnings which these people have

already wrought in the old order of things be our reply. Unbelievers have the ballot as well as Christians—that is the stubborn fact of the matter; and whether we deplore it or not, they will never consent to pay their money for the promulgation of Christian ideas.

But, suppose *them* to be in majority, and to fill the chairs of the state university with unbelieving doctors—John Fisk at the head, teaching metaphysics and ethics after Bain, Spencer, and Mill; John C. Draper and Youmans dividing natural science between them; prelections upon history delivered by a disciple of Buckle; and Auguste Compte *redevivus*, dean of all the faculties: Is it likely that Christian men will submit to paying taxes for such instruction?

Now it is not beyond belief that, should the government enter the domain of higher education, both these imbroglios might, in different states, become part of history within half a century. Not, however, while your system of state colleges is new. At the outset it would be imperative to conciliate all parties by compounding boards of instruction out of *all* sects and beliefs. Every faculty must be a religious mosaic. All attitudes to religion must be represented in it, in order that none may predominate. And now see the result. In studying the classics the pupil is taught by contrast the superiority of theistic and Christian notions of life. In physics, the very foundations of Christianity, and of theism, too, are gnawed away by the cankerous doctrines that matter and force are ultimate, and that man is a developed brute—a mere automaton. In one study the student is taught that induction rests on intuition; in another, that intuition is itself a product of induction; in ethics, that man is free and responsible; in history and political economy, that man is only a machine—nay, that his being a machine is the very reason why the sciences of history and political economy are possible. But who wants youthful minds trained in this most mischievous way? Such teaching would uproot in them the very idea of truth, and there are as yet none quite so radical as not to regard that a misfortune. Such misnamed education would offend believers and unbelievers alike, and a system of it could never be permanently supported by general taxation. Perhaps people are very foolish. That, I repeat, is not the question now. The point is, that people vote. We have committed ourselves to a republic, with its blessings and its ills. If the consignment of higher education to private hands is an ill, we must abide it. Right or wrong, wise or foolish, the great body of citizens will never, till the millennium at least, so agree in religion as to allow higher intellectual training to be administered by government.

But I said that to put higher education into political hands is not only impracticable, but also wrong in principle; and to this second point I request you now to attend. Denominational higher education, or higher education on private foundations, will prevail in our land, because the people will see that this, and this alone, is right. What is the business of the state? Is its function unlimited? May it do whatever a majority says it may do? Are majorities infallible? Are there not some things which even *they* have no right to do? It is high time that the attention of legislators was held to such queries as these. Much of our law-making is shockingly reckless of minority rights, and regardless of principles in general. If a measure will only pass, that fact, according to the regnant political philosophy of our time, is proof positive of its rightness. I believe that many advocates of state higher education are carried sheer away by the brilliancy and grandeur of the plan, not thinking or caring, perhaps, to ask whether there is legitimacy in it; inquiring only if it is possible. I am aware, however, that the abler pleaders for state establishments are careful to advance their grounds, and they generally affirm that the state must furnish this high culture in order to live. But for this, as I have said, they furnish not the remotest vestige of proof. I have sought for proof through all their writings to which I have had access, but to no avail. When we regard the number of great men, educators, jurists, law-makers, statesmen, editors, and writers, who have glorified our history without any college breeding, it is vain to deny that the government might survive and fulfil successfully all its real functions, though every college and university from Maine to California were razed level with the ground. Nor is the relation of colleges to common schools at all more essential.

The normal school, and not the college, is the proper complement to the common school. And normal schools it is the duty of the state to furnish. It is not true that the state will die without seeing to higher education.

Just here there is chance for an *argumentum ad hominem*. As observed already, government may abide without Christianity, or high learning either. Of the two, however, Christianity is infinitely the nearer to its life: for Christianity is now practically the only religion offerable to men, and no state ever yet endured long without religion, while many have stood centuries with low intellectual culture. Here, then, is religion with some appearance at least, of being vital to governmental stability. Here is higher education with confessedly less of such appearance. The reformers would deny the government's right to take charge of religion. They urge it to take charge of higher education. Their position is illogical. The government's attitude toward religion in this country is right, and it ought to hold the same attitude toward all those other such matters, which, though important enough to the highest weal of the people, and remotely so, perhaps, even to the nation's very existence, are, after all, *not vital* to the nation's existence.

The arguments of President White, and those who think with him, prove this and no more: that culture and liberal training are essential to the highest development and weal of the people, and this I believe as strongly as President White, or Mr. Adams, or any member of the Reichstag in Germany. Good universities, it is plain to all, advance a nation's intelligence and culture, increase the number of its great men, lift up its character, and promote the respect paid to it among the other nations of the earth.

But it is not the function of government to busy itself about the compassing of such ends as these. Its function is to protect the people in the exercise of their natural rights. It transcends its sphere putting hand to every scheme that can in any way advantage the people. It is none of the government's business how high or low a degree of literary culture the people possess, or what the nation's literary reputation is abroad, or to further discoveries in science, or to see to it that our national intelligence does not lag behind that of the age. Leave these things to individuals and to private societies, moved by their own tastes and convictions, and by the spirit of the times. Education in this higher aspect of it is too sacred a thing for the state to touch with its great, coarse, hard hands. Turn it over to those who have affinity for it, and will cultivate and foster it out of love. It is the only way in a republic like ours, in which learning can flourish, and it leaves government free to perform its only legitimate work, protecting the people in their natural rights.

This is one reason why I pronounce state meddling with higher education wrong, because this interest is utterly outside of government's legitimate activity.

Another point deserves to be considered. Religion is essential to the perfection of culture and intelligence, and the state cannot teach religion. If the people are unable to attain the desirable development without culture—and I am as earnest as any living man in maintaining that they are—then it is of prime consequence that their culture be of the choicest kind, and to be this, it must have the religious element. That the state can not impart this religious element so indispensable to true culture, is generally admitted, but the full breadth and bearing of the admission is not so generally understood. The government must be strictly, scrupulously, impartial in religion. So says the constitution of the United States. So also says precedent, extending back over half a century of our national history; and so, better than all, says the only true, abstract theory of state-craft. Disciples of Mohammed, of Confucius, of Buddha, devotees of every pagan cult, are as true citizens as Christians are. They are not to be *tolerated* on condition of conforming to all the Christian observances which we please to impose, but to be accorded their own inalienable God-given right of practicing religion as they see fit. It follows from this principle not only that the state may not teach Christianity as such, but that it may not even teach morality on Christian grounds. The furthest it can legitimately go in any religious direction, is to inculcate those common ideas of morality in which all agree, steadfastly refusing to decide upon their grounds.

Should the state in its public instructions go beyond this, and found morality in the nature or in the will of God, it would discriminate against a large class of citizens who do not so believe, and who have rights as well as Christians have. Often is it argued as if government were not bound to respect the religious views of such, but only to be neutral among the various sects of Christians. In reality, however, it is as criminally intolerant to discriminate against idolators in favor of Monotheists, as it would be to discriminate against Methodists in favor of Baptists. A man's creed has nothing whatever to do with his status as a citizen according to the American theory of government, and so, instruction given by the state cannot go beyond the simplest unsupported elements of morality without invading some citizen's rights.

The state laboring under such a restriction cannot be the provider of the best intellectual pabulum; it cannot furnish the inspiration needful for the highest intellectual attainments. Religion must be invoked; and the only religion worth invoking is Christianity.

Christianity is the native ally of intelligence. That Christian men should ever oppose intellectual progress, or that real unbelievers should ever attain pre-eminence in the same, are both very strange and anomalous facts. That they are facts, I will not deny; but they are abnormal—the outcome of peculiar conditions. Genuine and unadulterated Christianity cheers when science advances its standards. History presents to us the religion of the Cross marching at the very head and front of the world's educational forces. Civilization has never seen the like of it, in power, first, of creating in men a mental appetite, and then of filling their hungry minds with the most nutritious intellectual food. It is surprising and instructive to observe how soon the early Christians outstripped their pagan relatives and neighbors in the intellectual race. A love of letters seemed to be born in them at the same time with their faith. That whole age was one of research, of light. Nor did this light grow dim till Christianity became corrupted and the genuine preacher found a grave.

The renaissance came with the preacher's resurrection. Even

the infidel historian will tell you that intellectual quickening, as well as spiritual, waited upon the ministries of St. Francis and St. Dominic, and Tauler, and Huss, and Luther. Luther is remembered with as much honor to-day in his character of father to free thought, as he is in that of religious reformer. Rationalists, as well as Christians, love him. And with reason. To no other one man is Germany so much indebted for her present intellectual pre-eminence as to him; and it is well known that his bias in favor of active thought was the outcome of his faith. Nor is his influence, as a promoter of thinking, strange. Any man filled with the true spirit of the Christian religion will be a free-thinker in the better sense of the term; a lover of the truth, a searcher after it, an advocate of progress in thinking and knowledge. So of nations. It is the nations where Christianity has been least disseminated, where the preacher's voice has been longest and oftenest hushed, which have remained most backward mentally. Compare Germany with Italy, England with Spain, the United States with South America. The same is seen in heathen lands. No sooner have the seeds of religious truth sprung up there, than those peoples raise a clamor for schools. China and Japan in the same instant open their ears to hear the gospel, and their mouths to cry to Christian lands for teachers. It is not accidental that the great repositories of learning the world over, are of religious origin, and that scarcely a single broad and deep educational foundation has been laid in Christendom, except by the hands of Christian piety. And it is still worthier of remark, that it has been Christian people, stirred up by their faith to appreciate learning, who have demanded these institutions, and whose sons have filled them when erected.

Is it said that I have in these observations been misplacing cause and effect—that Christian ideas are only a few among ten thousand products of an advancing intelligence that is native to men? The reply is at hand, and it seems to me demonstrative. The Christian religion is, in its very nature, calculated to arouse and inspire the human intelligence. It is the natural nurse of great thoughts, of God, of man, of the world, of the world to come. It has even been charged upon Christianity as a fault, that she raises so many questions that she does not solve. It is at least one worthy office of such problems, that they furnish exercise-work to the mind of man such as nothing else can give. Other themes might, indeed, provoke activity in great and gifted minds. Religion comes home to the business and bosoms of all. It forces thought. There is nothing like it to set stationary minds agoing. Let Dr. Draper wax eloquent over the "sweetness and light" of Averroism, and the delectable culture that was bred in Moorish Spain by the doctrines of emanation and absorption. Where is Mohammedan culture to-day? Traverse Arabia and North Africa and inquire. Its very blood was poison, and needed only time to do its fatal work As well intellectually as spiritually was the Cross destined to outshine the Crescent. The fittest has survived. It is not religion alone that has occasion to weep over the monistic tendencies of these times. Literature, philosophy, art—all culture, are equally concerned. Let the belief gain general prevalence that there is no spiritual world, no living God, no immortality, and those who will then regard intellectual attainment worth its cost will be few indeed. Religion will not depart from this world alone. When you compose her form in death, prepare tears for other objects of love, many and dear. Art, literature, culture, and religion have taken oath to die and be buried as they have lived, locked in each other's arms.

I need not pursue this thought. I protest against divorcing education from religion. They are the proper complements of each other. To education without religion that dignified title does not belong. It is the form without the power. A state system of education, into which religion cannot enter, is wrong in principle. It deserves as little the support of those who are interested in the intellectual, as of those who are interested in the religious welfare of the people.

But, if secular education cannot adequately form the mind, still less—and this is my last reason for calling it wrong in theory—can it yield character. The principle is general, but its application is especially striking in our own land and time. A strong moral character is the deepest need of the American people to-day; and every one knows that the intellectual class has a mighty power in fixing the character of society at large. The religious tone of our college teaching is almost as important in this regard, as that of our preaching itself. If the great mass of our American college graduates can go forth to their life-work, each possessed of an iron moral principle begotten and matured in four years of theistic teaching, the power of these institutions for moral good will pass all reckoning. They will be to our people like perpetual smiles from on high. If the same amount of intelligence enters public life, purely secular, with only such ideas of morals as it can imbibe with the state for its preceptor, it can hardly avoid being a curse. Thus far college instruction, with its pronounced theistic bent, has stood in the front rank of agencies for conserving and advancing morality. We cannot spare so salubrious an influence now. We are seeing enough of the ill that results from secularism, in the common schools. It is the painful conviction, I believe, of every morally thoughtful man, that these schools are not producers of high character. Theoretically the Catholics are right, that even here education should not be non-religious. Government, however, being indispensable, and these schools being indispensable to government, and it being impos sible in a free republic for them to teach religion, the theory must suffer, and we must do our best to preserve the symmetry of lower education by diligent Sunday-school and home instruction.

But, a further divorce between education and religion is not necessary, and should be fought against to the last. Besides the minor infelicities always arising from a weak state of the public conscience, there are several towering evils which torment us now, that can only be remedied by a better moral sense in the great public breast. An earnest cry is rising from all quarters for a higher sense of honor in society. The demand is just. It is to be feared that honor is less a living force among us than in any other civilized people. Now, the dulness of this feeling is an evil sign in respect to our morality. It indicates that even such of our conduct as does accord with the moral law may not be moral. For "honor is not something beside and above morality, but belongs to it most intimately. Its field lies between the coarser and more obvious requirements of justice and the self-forgetting impulses of love."* Honor is only morality's "consummate flower." Would we have more of it? Assuredly we need more. Let us cultivate morality more assiduously, and urge it forward to ripeness. Weakness in moral conviction can never be cured by mere exhortation and appeal. The moral sense must be trained. Any agency that can aid in effecting this is beyond price.

There are more conspicuous evils which, so far as I can see, are out of the reach of all other remedies than this of which I speak. They are only to be crushed by the weight of the people's moral conviction uttered against them. I instance incorporate avarice, that so largely controls legislation, and makes laws by which the people are defrauded. Yes, even if each law-maker is a Solon for wisdom and an Aristides for justice, the evil remains. Laws can not be specific; and cases must often arise under the best of laws where adroit corporations, without breaking any fiat written upon statute-books, can get the people at a disadvantage and rob them. Where is the remedy? The ballot-box says: "It is not in me." The legislature says: "It is not in me." The courts say: "We have heard the fame thereof with our ears, but we possess not the cure." There is no cure but in a toning up of the pnblic conscience. Let the members of corporations know that all the people, empanelled as a jury and sworn upon the Bible by a stern conscience, will try them individually, and bring them in guilty whenever they step over the bounds of equity, and even a corporation of fiends will be cautious. There is something awfully commanding in the rebuke of a nation's conscience. Men cannot brave it. Devils cannot. We saw its power when Congress wrongly voted to enrich itself at our expense, and when corruption grew fat in the high places of New York city by feeding upon the people's wealth. Here is our security—our only security against such abuses—a better conscience in the popular bosom.

Intemperance is another of these dreadful demons that law cannot exorcise, but an Herculean conscience can. There are still others, and their name is legion. It is of indescribable conse-

* President Woolsey in his address at Harvard College in 1875.

quence to our proper development as a people that every thing possible be done to elevate public morals; and when I reflect upon the commanding position of intelligence among the social forces, I have no words to express my anxiety that all the intelligence in our country may be of such a character as to prove an ally to morality. Let light be made the medium of warmth; let the two fall upon men in blended rays as they come forth from God, the eternal Sun and Source of both. For this saving admixture of light and heat there can be no better conductor to the souls of this or of any other nation, than sanctified collegiate instruction.

Thus, friends, you have my convictions about the destiny of the denominational college. It will live, and it will be the great educational machine of America's future. It will, because it must be so; it will, because the people will judge that it ought to be so. No greater work confronts the Baptist people of to-day, whether as citizens or as Christians, than the proper endowment of Denison University. For what it has cost, our college has no superior in the land. Still, its needs are great and sore—new professors, new apparatus, new buildings. With gratitude to God for past providence, and a firm reliance upon His sovereign help and headship for the future, let us deeply vow that the plaintive cry of this beloved seat of learning shall not be heard in vain. If, in us, the coming years shall find the same heroic devotion to its interests that fatally animated the translated and immortal man to whose office I, this night, unworthily succeed, the College *will* not cry in vain.

www.ingramcontent.com/pod-product-compliance
Lightning Source LLC
LaVergne TN
LVHW011146110826
845150LV00008B/2536

* 9 7 8 1 4 1 8 1 9 1 6 9 6 *